Learn Microservices - ASP.NET Core and Docker

Be ready for coding away next week

Arnaud Weil

Learn Microservices - ASP.NET Core and Docker

Be ready for coding away next week

Arnaud Weil

ISBN 978-0-244-40291-4

To my parents, for teaching me freedom and making sure I can enjoy it.

To my wonderful family. Your love and support fueled this book.

To my readers who suggested improvements to this book, especially Doğan Kartaltepe.

Contents

Introduction

What this book is not

I made my best to keep this book small, so that you can learn microservices quickly without getting lost in petty details. If you are looking for a reference book where you'll find answers to all the questions you may have within the next 4 years of your microservices practice, you'll find other heavy books for that.

My purpose is to swiftly provide you with the tools you need to code your first microservice application using Docker and ASP.NET Core, then be able to look for more by yourself when needed. While some authors seem to pride themselves in having the thickest book, in this series I'm glad I achieved the thinnest possible book for my purpose. Though I tried my best to keep all of what seems necessary, based on my 16 years experience of teaching .NET.

I assume that you know what microservices are and when to use them. In case you don't, read the following *Why microservices* chapter.

Prerequisites

In order for this book to meet its goals, you must:

- Have basic experience creating applications with C#
- Know what a Web application is

How to read this book

This book's aim is to make you productive as quickly as possible. For this we'll use some theory, several demonstrations, plus exercises. Exercises appear like the following:

 Do it yourself: Time to grab your keyboard and code away to meet the given objectives.

Tools you need

The only tools you'll need to work through this book are the following:

- Windows 10
- Visual Studio 2017 (Community, Professional or Enterprise)

- Docker 17.09 or higher (Community)

When installing Visual Studio, make sure you select the *ASP.NET* and *.NET Core* components.

Source code

All of the source code for the demos and do-it-yourself solutions is available at https://bitbucket.org/epobb/microservicesexercises

It can be downloaded as a ZIP file[1], or if you installed GIT you can simply type:

```
git clone https://bitbucket.org/epobb/microservicesexer\
cises.git
```

---

1. Why microservices?

If you're in a hurry, you can safely skip this chapter and head straight to the Microservices as seen from the client chapter. This *Why microservices* chapter is there for those that want to know why microservices should be used.

1.1 What are they?

Microservices are an architectural solution to several challenges faced by modern software. Among other things, they help solve either of the following requirements:

- over time there may be several front-ends for similar business processes (thick clients, SPAs, mobile applications, IoT devices, ...), some of which unpredicted;
- applications may be hosted on-premises or in a Cloud infrastructure;
- applications should be resilient: they should remain available when outages occur over parts of its components;
- applications should be able to scale up: when demand is high it should be possible to run them over

several machines in order to handle each request faster;

- applications should allow for replications, i.e., having duplicates across different machines or data centers so that computing power outage doesn't make them unavailable;
- large teams working on the same application should be able to work as independently as possible;
- future applications are likely to interact with a part of the application you are building.

In order to achieve such goals, microservices' architectures split an application into smaller blocks. If you've been architecting applications correctly you probably already separated your application code in projects, but that still makes for one big monolithic application.

A monolithic application bundles its pieces together into a single unit. that cannot easily meet the requirements expressed above. Here's what a fictitious monolithic application could look like:

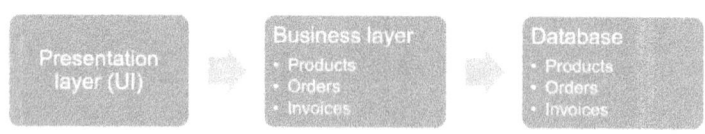

On the positive side, a monolithic application is easy to code and deploy.

In order to meet the requirements expressed earlier, a microservice architecture splits the application into several services. The following could be a microservice architecture corresponding to the monolithic application shown above:

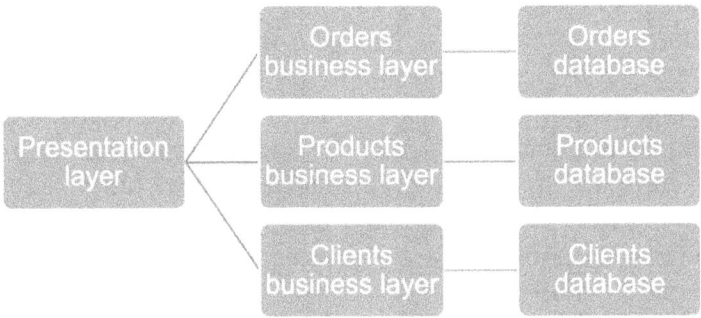

How you split the functionality can be debated. It is generally good practice to make sure each service meets a functional need of its own.

1.2 Microservices induce complexity

Services are likely to depend on each other; which doesn't appear in the schema above. For instance, considering the application above an order would most probably reference a client and several products. Which brings some questions like *how do services reference each other?* There are answers for that depending on what needs to be achieved. For instance there may be a service-discovery service, or a mediation layer.

This is just an example of the complexity that a microservice architecture brings. We'll see more later but the scope of this book is not to cover it all, especially since there are potentially many answers to each problem.

What I want you to understand is that a microservice architecture is nothing simple. As the needs grow, the complexity will grow faster than in an equivalent monolithic architecture. My advice: use microservice architecture when you need to meet requirements like the ones listed at the beginning of that chapter. Otherwise keep with monolithic architectures, be it a service-based monolithic architecture.

Anyway, my point is about complexity not impossibility. There's a lot of awesome tooling out there today that makes a microservice architecture much easier to code, assemble and deploy. We'll see some of them in this book.

2. Microservices as seen from the client

A microservice architecture is made of services. Those services handle HTTP communication that request or send data. In case you're familiar with this, you can head straight to the exercise. Otherwise, let's review the fundamentals so you can build your knowledge over solid basis.

2.1 HTTP

Services, whether they are microservices or not, are usually called over HTTP. Here's the schema of an HTTP request:

A *client* sends a request to a *server*. The client may be a mobile application, an IoT object, a SPA application

(Angular, React, ...) or whatever you please - including another service. By the way, services will be calling each other in a microservice architecture. The server is what you code, and it contains the business logic.

HTTP in itself is pretty simple. It's a text-based protocol where the client:

1. opens a TCP connection to the server;
2. sends data (the *request*, see below) to the server;
3. receives data (the *response*, see below) from the server;
4. closes the connection.

The request is made of two parts: headers and possibly data, separated by a blank line (did I tell you HTTP was simple?). It may look like that:

```
GET /index HTTP/1.1
Host: www.mysite.com
```

In the above example there is one single header (Host) and no data. The first line states a *verb*, a URL, and the version of the HTTP protocol being used. The verb corresponds to what the client wants to do, for instance:

- GET is used to fetch data without modifying server data
- POST is used to update server data
- DELETE is used to - ahem! - delete server data, or at least request deletion.

GET requests do not contain a data payload in the request since the headers and URL are sufficient, but the other types of requests contain data. Here's an example POST request, but an UPDATE request would look similar:

```
POST http://server:51426/api/TrainSchedules HTTP/1.1
Content-Type: application/json
Host: server:51426
Content-Length: 94

{"departureTime":"2018-04-03T21:56:48.6711219+01:00","d\
istanceKm":1054,"destination":"Berlin"}
```

The payload here is JSON, a widely used format for services as we'll see very soon.

The server processes the request and returns a response using the same TCP connection that was used for the request. That TCP connection is then closed. Here's an example response:

```
HTTP/1.1 200 OK
Content-Type: text/html
Content-Length: 81

<html>
    <body>
        <p>Welcome to our site</p>
    </body>
</html>
```

Just like the request, the response is made up of two parts: headers and possibly data, separated by a blank line. Plus a first line that confirms the protocol and provides a status code and message. The status code's first digit is the most important: 2 means everything was alright, 4 means there was a problem processing the request (you know, that ubiquitous *404 Not found*).

There can be many more headers. In the above example you can see the two headers that are commonly used in responses. *Content-Type* tells the client how the data (what comes below the blank line) should be interpreted. It's a MIME type. MIME types are well established[1]. Though there are many possible MIME types, only some of them are used for services.

2.2 Payloads

We are focusing on services, right? A (micro)service is mostly used for computer-computer interaction, so it needs a MIME type that's appropriate for its payloads (the data that is sent in requests and received in responses).

Extensive work from the OASIS consortium in order to standardize services at the beginning of the century (wow, that sounds *so vintage*) established the XML format for payloads; the consortium even wrapped it into the SOAP standard (which is made of XML). So services

---

[1] https://www.iana.org/assignments/media-types/media-types.xhtml

used the *text/xml* MIME type for quite a while, and many still do.

Then came SPA applications (Angular, React and the likes), which became widely used endpoints for user consumption of services. Those applications run in the browser using JavaScript that happens to suck at XML processing. Sure, JavaScript can parse and produce XML, but it's a painful process for it. What JavaScript can easily parse and produce is its own format: JSON. Since JSON is as easily read by humans as XML and less verbose, it quickly became the norm for services.

So that's where we stand today: (micro)services use mainly JSON as their payload format for requests and answers, plus XML sometimes.

2.3 Do you speak JSON

If you aren't familiar with JSON, don't worry: it can be learnt very quickly. Think of it as anonymous C# objects. For instance, consider the following declaration:

```
var myObject = new() {
  Foo = "bar",
  Value = 5.5,
  Really = true
}
```

This anonymous object instantiation in C# is almost

JSON. Let's replace the equal signs with semicolons, and wrap property names with quotes. This is what we get:

```
var myObject = new() {
  "Foo": "bar",
  "Value": 5.5,
  "Really": true
}
```

We're almost there. We currently have an hybrid C#-JSON code. Now let's remove the variable declaration and call to *new* since they don't describe a value (they describe what we want to do with the value). This is what we get:

```
{
  "Foo": "bar",
  "Value": 5.5,
  "Really": true
}
```

Guess what? This is valid JSON. It simply represents the data for an object that has 3 properties.

Now suppose you want to describe an array of object values: all you need to do is use brackets around them. And line returns count as spaces. Yes, all just like C#. Here's one such array:

```
[
  { "Foo": "bar", "Value": 5.5, "Really": true },
  { "Foo": "tball", "Value": 2.3, "Really": false }
]
```

That's almost all there is to JSON. I could show an example of a complex property value, but that would be just recursive use of the first sample and I'll spare you that.

2.4 Client types

Once a (micro)service is published and listens over HTTP (that's what we'll do in this book), many different types of clients can consume it:

- heavy clients like UWP, WPF, Windows Forms;
- browsers using SPA applications like Angular, React, Vue.js, Knockout or jQuery, or even plain JavaScript
- mobile applications;
- IoT devices, e.g. your fridge ordering milk when it senses you'll soon be running out of milk;
- other services, which makes for a services-based architecture;
- utilities like command-line applications.

In this book you'll use WPF, command-line and services as the clients of your services.

2.5 Manual testing

Once you start building a microservice, you'll want to test it. A microservice usually has no user interface, hence testing requires you to send HTTP requests and check for the response.

> That way of interacting with a service (HTTP) is often called an API for Application Programming Interface.

An obvious tool is your browser. When you type a URL in the address bar, your browser issues an *HTTP GET* request to that URL. Downside: you have no control over the headers it sends. Which means that you really need another tool.

Good news: there are many tools out there that will enable you to issue HTTP requests like *Fiddler* or *Postman*. You can go on and use any tool you like really; for simplicity sake in this book we'll use the *Invoke-WebRequest* command that is part of PowerShell since it's already present on your Windows machine. If you're using a Linux-based machine, you can use the *curl* command. Even PowerShell accepts the *curl* command (and maps it to its *Invoke-WebRequest* command).

Suppose you want to make the following HTTP request: *GET http://someserver/api*

You could issue the following PowerShell command:

```
Invoke-WebRequest http://someserver/api
```

This is the actual HTTP request that gets issued:

```
GET http://someserver/api HTTP/1.1
User-Agent: Mozilla/5.0 (Windows NT; Windows NT 10.0; f\
r-FR) WindowsPowerShell/5.1.16299.98
Host: someserver
Proxy-Connection: Keep-Alive
```

You aren't required to provide other parameters since *GET* is the default HTTP verb used by the *Invoke-WebRequest* command. The response is provided in full details, but if you are interested only in the data payload, you may get the *Content* property from the result:

```
(Invoke-WebRequest http://someserver/api).Content
```

When you need to use a verb other than *GET* you'll surely need to send data. The *Invoke-WebRequest* command allows you to provide your data using the *Body* parameter and the verb to be used is passed through the *Method* parameter.

```
Invoke-WebRequest -Method POST -Body '{"foo":"bar","val\
ue":10}' -Header @{"Content-Type"="application/json"} h\
ttp://someserver/api
```

Note that in the command above we're also sending a *Content-Type* header in order to tell the server that we're using JSON as the payload data format - this depends on the specific API you call.

This is the actual HTTP request that gets issued when the command above is executed:

```
POST http://someserver/api HTTP/1.1
Content-Type: application/json
User-Agent: Mozilla/5.0 (Windows NT; Windows NT 10.0; f\
r-FR) WindowsPowerShell/5.1.16299.98
Host: someserver
Content-Length: 24

{"foo":"bar","value":10}
```

Let's try this on a real-world example.

2.6 Exercise - Invoke a microservice manually

 Using PowerShell, make an HTTP GET request to the service located at the following URL:

```
https://en.wikipedia.org/w/api.php?action=query&format=\
json&prop=info&list=allpages
```

2.7 Exercise solution

- From a PowerShell command-line, type the following and check the returned *Content*:

```
Invoke-WebRequest "https://en.wikipedia.org/w/api.php?a\
ction=query&format=json&prop=info&list=allpages"
```

- Make sure the HTTP response status code is *200 OK*.

3. Microservices server-side

3.1 About coding the server

We saw in the previous chapter how a client consumes a microservice using HTTP. Now is time to code the server-hosted microservice.

Since clients are going to issue HTTP requests, a microservice is basically a piece of software that serves those requests. Which is very simple: all it needs to do is listen on a given TCP port, process the incoming HTTP message, and output a corresponding HTTP response. Since HTTP is plain text, a microservice may be coded with a few lines of code.

3.2 There comes .NET Core

Virtually any software stack can process incoming HTTP requests and thus be a microservice. There are full-blown SaaS solutions available, but this book is about coding your own microservice, which means coding your own business rules. Many server technology stacks may be

used, but since you are reading this book chances are
that .NET Core was selected.

If you want to learn ASP.NET Core in full depth, you may
read my Learn ASP.NET Core MVC[1] book. However I don't
want you to read two books when one is enough and your
time is precious, so I'm going to provide you with the
essential knowledge needed for creating microservices
using .NET Core.

3.3 Introduction to ASP.NET Core

.NET Core includes ASP.NET Core, which in turn includes
an out-of-the box HTTP server named Kestrel. Kestrel can
be instantiated with one line of code. HTTP requests may
be served using a few more lines of code. In fact, here
is a full-blown JSON-based microservice coded using
ASP.NET Core:

```
public class Program
{
    public static void Main(string[] args)
    {
        var host = WebHost.CreateDefaultBuilder(args)
            .UseKestrel()
            .UseStartup<Startup>()
            .Build();

        host.Run();
```

---
[1] https://leanpub.com/netcore

```
    }
}

public class Startup
{
  public void Configure(IApplicationBuilder app)
  {
    app.Run(async (context) =>
    {
      await context.Response.WriteAsync(
        "{ \"message\": \"Hello World!\" }");
    });
  }
}
```

From there you could parse the incoming HTTP request using the provided *Request* property from the *context* parameter and live happily ever after. For very small needs, that's it. For more important needs, you know that an adequate software architecture is necessary. The MVC Web API framework provides us with a software architecture that's suited for creating microservices. ASP.NET Core MVC Web API is part of ASP.NET Core MVC, and insures you create unit-testable microservices where concerns are clearly separated.

3.4 ASP.NET Core Web API

Project structure

Hopefully Visual Studio comes with a Web API starter template. Although there isn't much to add to the pre-vious code in order to get it going, I'd rather not have you stumble upon problems caused by a misplaced code line. Let me show you.

I'm going to start Visual Studio and create a new project using the *ASP.NET Core Web Application* template. Once I validate my settings, I get a *New ASP.NET Core Web Application* dialog box where I select the *Web Application (Model-View-Controler)* template:

Although there is a *Web API* project template, I'd rather select the *Web Application (Model-View-Controler)*. In case you wonder, it's just a matter of which starter files Visual Studio provides me with. I could add a Web API to either project type. The reason why I specifically select the *Web Application (Model-View-Controller)* template is that this starter template makes it easier to add scaffolded views (i.e. HTML rendering for an end-user). Not a necessity, but that's something I want to do later in that book.

You may want to take a peek at the various files created, but that's not necessary. As of now, all of our work is going to happen in the *Controllers* folder. Controllers are the abstraction that ASP.NET Core MVC uses in order to represent the fact that we handle an incoming HTTP request and serve it with a response; which is exactly what we want to do when we code an API.

Controllers, actions and routes

Let's create a service that returns a weather forecast to the client. I'd like the client to issue the following HTTP request when they want to get the weather forecast in Seattle:

```
GET http://<server>/api/forecast/city/Seattle
```

In ASP.NET Core Web API, that request is handled by a method. Which makes it really simple. For each HTTP request (same verb and URL), we're going to write a method. Methods that will handle similar URLs will be grouped into classes. And that's about it.

But wait. What if your boss discovers that your work is actually that easy? Don't worry, the ASP.NET Core team thought about it and instead of calling those methods, classes and URLs they used more nerdy words: actions, controllers and routes. So instead of having to admit that your work is about writing classes that contain methods which handle URLs, you can say that your highy-skilled work is about writing controllers that contain actions which handle routes.

So I'm going to add a class - well, a *controller*. I right-click the *Controllers* directory from the *Solution Explorer* and select *Add / Controller...* from the contextual menu. From the resulting *Add Scaffold* dialog I select *API Controller - Empty* selection and click the *Add* button.

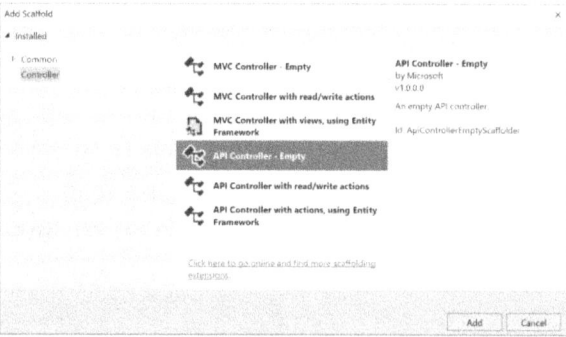

I get an *Add Empty API Controller* dialog asking me the controller name. I name it *WeatherController*.

Take a look at the generated code. It's really simple:

```
[Produces("application/json")]
[Route("api/Weather")]
public class WeatherController : Controller
{
}
```

Nothing tricky here. Just note that the controller inherits from a *Controller* class and there's a *Route* attribute stating which URLs this controller is going to handle. The *Produces* attribute could be omitted. It states that any client will receive a JSON response no matter what content type it requests.

Since I want to handle an HTTP request, I need to write a method - oh, sorry - an *action*. Here is the resulting code:

```
[Produces("application/json")]
[Route("api/forecast")]
public class WeatherController : Controller
{
  [Route("city/:name")]
  public string CityForecast(string name)
  {
    switch (DateTime.Now.Second%3)
    {
      case 0:
        return "Sunny";
      case 1:
        return "Cloudy";
      case 2:
      default:
        return "Rainy";
```

```
    }
  }
}
```

Note that I changed the *Route* attribute on the controller, since it didn't fit the API URL I want to expose.

The two *Route* attributes (the one on the action and the one on the controller) combine in order to describe the full route that an action handles. That comes in handy since routes that belong to the same controller are likely to share a common root.

The *Route* attribute on the action contains a parameter: the *name* parameter of the method will be extracted from the URL where the :name placeholder is.

Complex return types

Actions can return complex types, that will be converted to the required output format (JSON here, since that's what the *Produces* attribute states). For instance, I could return both a textual description and low/high temperatures.

First, I add the following class in the *Models* folder:

```
public class WeatherForecast
{
  public string Description { get; set; }
  public double Low { get; set; }
  public double High { get; set; }
}
```

Placing such a class in the *Models* folder simply is a convention. We could add it elsewhere, but remember that one of the driving reasons for selecting MVC is having a predictable project structure.

Here's our modified action:

```
[Route("city/:name")]
public WeatherForecast WeatherForecast(string name)
{
  var r = new Random(DateTime.Now.Millisecond);

  double low = r.NextDouble() * 15 - 5;
  double high = low + r.NextDouble() * 15;
  string description;

  switch (DateTime.Now.Second % 3)
  {
    case 0:
      description = "Sunny";
      break;
    case 1:
      description = "Cloudy";
      break;
    case 2:
```

```
    default:
      description ="Rainy";
      break;
  }
  return new WeatherForecast()
  {
    Description = description,
    Low = low,
    High = high
  };
}
```

Got it? Please show me with the following exercise.

3.5 Exercise - Create a train scheduling service

 Create a new micro service named *ScheduleService* using the *ASP.NET Core Web Application* template. Your project should use *ASP.NET Core 2.0* and the *Web Application (Model-View-Controler)* template.

Your microservice should listen on the following URL: http://localhost:[port]/api/NextDeparture

When that URL is invoked, your microservice should return JSON that appears like:

```
{"departureTime":"2018-01-03T21:56:48.6711219+01:00","n\
umber":"5423","destination":"Paris"}
```

3.6 Exercise solution

- Start Visual Studio.
- Click on the *File / New / Project...* menu entry.
- In the *New Project* dialog box, select the *ASP.NET Core Web Application* template making sure that you select *Templates / Visual C# / .NET Core* on the left-hand side. In the *Name* zone at the bottom, type "ScheduleService". Click the *OK* button.
- In the *New ASP.NET Core Web Application* dialog box, select the *.NET Core* and *ASP.NET Core 2.0* at the top. Select the *Web Application (Model-View-Controler)* template in the middle. Make sure the *Enable Docker Support* checkbox is unchecked. Click the *OK* button.
- Open the *Solution Explorer* clicking on the *View / Solution Explorer* menu entry.
- In the *Solution Explorer*, right-click the *Controllers* directory, and select *Add / Controller...* from the context menu.
- In the *Add Scaffold* dialog box, select the *API Controller - Empty* template. Click the *Add* button.
- In the *Add Empty API Controller* dialog box, type *NextDepartureController* as the controller name. Click the *Add* button.
- Locate the following code:

```
[Produces("application/json")]
[Route("api/NextDeparture")]
public class NextDepartureController : Controller
{
}
```

- Replace it with the following code:

```
[Produces("application/json")]
[Route("api/NextDeparture")]
public class NextDepartureController : Controller
{
  public IActionResult GetNext()
  {
    return Ok(new {
      DepartureTime = DateTime.Now.AddMinutes(50),
      Number = "5423",
      Destination = "Paris"
    });
  }
}
```

- From the *Debug* menu click *Start Without Debugging*
- Point your browser to the following URL (port number varies):

http://localhost:51426/api/NextDeparture

- From a PowerShell command-line, type the following and check the returned *Content*:

```
Invoke-WebRequest http://localhost:51426/api/NextDepart\
ure
```

4. Database access using Entity Framework Core

4.1 Introduction to Entity Framework Core

ASP.NET Core offers an ORM that can be easily used for accessing relational databases like SQL Server or MySQL: Entity Framework Core. In an architecture where we want to keep our microservices simple, Entity Framework Core makes a great tool.

Another nifty thing about Entity Framework Core is that it can store data in a real relational database or in-memory without changing your code: all it takes is a little changes in the Startup configuration. This is great for agile development where you want to start quickly (in-memory) but may need to use a relational database later on.

Just in case you aren't familiar with Entity Framework, I'm going to quickly explain how to get running using Entity Framework Code First.

Entity Framework provides object-relational mapping. That is, it can save you the hassle of writing most of your data-access code. It is based on providers that actually handle the data access like *InMemory* (for testing purposes) or *SqlServer*.

In the simplest scenario, we code one class for each table in a database. Let's code a `Car` class:

```
public class Car
{
  public int ID { get; set; }
  public string Model { get; set; }
  public double MaxSpeed { get; set; }
}
```

In order to access a database we need a *context* class. A class on which to we call methods that get and update the data from the database. Such classes are typically named *CarFactory* or *DataFactory*, or even *DataAccess*.

Easily done using Entity Framework: all we have to do is inherit from the `DbContext` class and add one property for each table, typed as `DbSet<T>`. In our example that would be:

```
public class GarageFactory : DbContext
{
    public DbSet<Car> Cars { get; set; }
    // add any other table here
}
```

Since our MVC application gets its services injected, let's ensure a *GarageFactory* instance will be available for controllers that need data access. This needs two steps:

1. add a constructor to *GarageFactory* class that gets options;
2. register *GarageFactory* during dependency injection setup, that is in Startup.ConfigureServices.

> As stated earlier, our goal here is not to dig deep into ASP.NET Core and we have enough to get you going. Should you want to learn more about Entity Framework Core and dependency injection, please refer to Learn ASP.NET Core MVC[a] book.
>
> [a]https://leanpub.com/netcore

Here is the overloaded constructor we need to add, even if empty:

```
public class GarageFactory : DbContext
{
  public GarageFactory
    DbContextOptions<GarageFactory> options)
  : base(options) { }

    public DbSet<Car> Cars { get; set; }
}
```

Next we need to configure dependency injection for our *GarageFactory* class. I need to add the following using directive to the top of the Startup.cs file:

```
using Microsoft.EntityFrameworkCore;
```

And here is the code to be added to the *Startup.ConfigureServices* method:

```
services.AddDbContext<GarageFactory>(
  options => options.UseInMemoryDatabase("Garage")
);
```

That's all there is to it. Our in-memory database is ready to be used all through our service. If you got everything right, you know that all we need now in order to provide an HTTP API access to our database is to create a controller with the necessary actions.

4.2 Scaffold your code and save time

I believe that a good developer is lazy. Lazy enough to code as little as possible. But what if you're lazier and don't even want to code what's necessary? That's where Visual Studio scaffolding can help. Let me show you how we get it to actually write a controller that exposes the *Cars* table of our database.

First step is to build the project (select *Build / Build Solution* from the menu). Next, from the *Solution Explorer* I right-click the *Controllers* folder and select *Add / Controller...* from the contextual menu. In the *Add Scaffold* dialog box I select *API Controller with actions, using Entity Framework* and click the *Add* button:

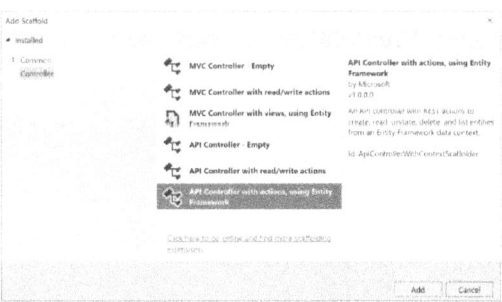

An *Add API Controller with actions, using Entity Framework* dialog box opens. I select *Car* as the *Model class* and *GarageFactory* as the *Data context class*, keep the proposed controller name and click the *Add* button.

Let's have a look at the code that was just scaffolded. The class declaration and attributes come with no surprise:

```
[Produces("application/json")]
[Route("api/Cars")]
public class CarsController : Controller
{
   ...
}
```

According to the *Route* attributes, all actions on the *Cars* table will be done making HTTP requests to the following URL, simply changing the HTTP verb:

```
http://<server>/api/Cars
```

The private field and constructor may surprise you in case you aren't familiar with dependency injection:

```
private readonly GarageFactory _context;

public CarsController(GarageFactory context)
{
    _context = context;
}
```

Nothing strange just pure goodness: the *CarsController* class is simply stating that whenever it is instantiated it should receive an instance of the *GarageFactory* class. Pure goodness since it means you don't need to worry there about how the *GarageFactory* will be instantiated. Who decides, you say? The *Startup.ConfigureServices* method when it calls the *services.AddDbContext*.

Each method in the *CarsController* class is an action that states what how each HTTP verb will be handled. The *GET* method on */api/Cars* is a no-brainer:

```
[HttpGet]
public IEnumerable<Car> GetCars()
{
  return _context.Cars;
}
```

Fetch all the rows from the Cars table and return them. Just that simple. I won't go over each method since they all look quite similar; let's just examine the one that handles the *POST* method on */api/Cars*:

```
[HttpPost]
public async Task<IActionResult> PostCar([FromBody] Car\
 car)
{
  if (!ModelState.IsValid)
  {
    return BadRequest(ModelState);
  }

  _context.Cars.Add(car);
  await _context.SaveChangesAsync();
```

```
return CreatedAtAction("GetCar", new { id = car.ID },\
car);
}
```

The *FromBody* attribute on the *car* parameter ensures that the car properties will be taken from the body of the HTTP response, not from the query string or some other place. The call to the *ModelState.IsValid* method simply ensures that any data annotation attribute[1] stated on the *Car* class are respected by the data you got over HTTP.

Note that the return types are provided through calls to the controller *BadRequest* and *CreatedAtAction* methods. Those methods return types that are simple wrappers providing standard HTTP response codes and messages. In order to be able to return any of them, the return type of the action method has been set to *IActionResult*. Using such return types, in case you want to return your own business object instance just use the *Ok(object)* method.

So much for the theory: let's practice.

---

[1] Like *Required*, those attributes can be found in the System.ComponentModel.DataAnnotations namespace.

4.3 Exercise - Extend the train scheduling service

 We want to extend the *ScheduleService* microservice so that it can store train schedules: their departure time, destination, and the distance in Kilometers of the ride.

Add a *TrainSchedule* class with the following properties:

Name	Type
ID	Guid
DepartureTime	DateTime
Destination	string
DistanceKm	int

Create an Entity Framework data context that stores *TrainSchedule* entries in-memory. Use Visual Studio scaffolding to create a JSON API based on your data context that exposes CRUD operations on *TrainSchedule*.

4.4 Exercise solution

- In the *Solution Explorer*, right-click the *Models* directory, and select *Add / Class...* from the context menu.

- In the *Add New Item* dialog box, type *TrainSchedule* in the *Name* field. Click the *Add* button.
- Locate the following code:

```
public class TrainSchedule
{
}
```

- Replace it with the following code:

```
public class TrainSchedule
{
  public Guid ID { get; set; }
  public DateTime DepartureTime { get; set; }
  public string Destination { get; set; }
  public int DistanceKm { get; set; }
}
```

- In the *Solution Explorer*, right-click the *Schedule-Service* project (not the solution) and select *Add / New folder*. Rename the created folder to *Services*.
- In the *Solution Explorer*, right-click the *Services* folder, and select *Add / Class...* from the context menu.
- In the *Add New Item* dialog box, type *TrainsDbContext* in the *Name* field. Click the *Add* button.
- Add the following code at the top of the file:

```
using Microsoft.EntityFrameworkCore;
using ScheduleService.Models;
```

- Locate the following code:

```
public class TrainsDbContext
{
}
```

- Replace it with the following code:

```
public class TrainsDbContext : DbContext
{
  public TrainsDbContext(
      DbContextOptions<TrainsDbContext> options
  ) . base(options) { }

  public DbSet<TrainSchedule> Schedules { get; set; }
}
```

- Open the *Startup.cs* file and add the following code to the top of the file:

```
using Microsoft.EntityFrameworkCore;
using ScheduleService.Services;
```

- In the *Startup* class, add the following code to the top of the *ConfigureServices* method:

```
services.AddDbContext<TrainsDbContext>(options =>
    options.UseInMemoryDatabase("trains"));
```

- From the *Build* menu click *Build Solution*
- In the *Solution Explorer*, right-click the *Controllers* directory, and select *Add / Controller...* from the context menu.
- In the *Add Scaffold* dialog box, select the *API Controller with actions, using Entity Framework* template. Click the *Add* button.
- In the *Add API Controller with actions, using Entity Framework* dialog box, enter the following values:
  - Model class: TrainSchedule (ScheduleService.Models)
  - Data context class: TrainsDbContext (ScheduleService.Data)
  - Controller name: TrainSchedulesController
- Click the *Add* button.
- From the *Debug* menu click *Start Without Debugging*
- From a PowerShell command-line, type the following command:

```
(Invoke-WebRequest http://localhost:51426/api/TrainSche\
dules).Content
```

- Check that the returned value is an empty array:

```
[]
```

- From a PowerShell command-line, type the following command:

```
Invoke-WebRequest -Method POST -Body '{"departureTime":\
"2018-04-03T21:56:48.6711219+01:00","distanceKm":1054,"\
destination":"Berlin"}' -Header @{"Content-Type"="appli\
cation/json"} http://localhost:51426/api/TrainSchedules
```

- Check that the returned *StatusDescription* is *Created*.
- From a PowerShell command-line, type the following command:

```
(Invoke-WebRequest http://localhost:51426/api/TrainSche\
dules).Content
```

- Check that the returned value is an array containing the schedule you just created.

5. Adding UI server-side

5.1 To UI or not to UI

Microservices are bound to be called by other microservices or other machines (like an IoT garden mower). In case an end-user wants to interact with a microservice, she usually does so through a client software that suits her and her system: a mobile application on a smartphone, an Angular or React web application in a browser, a WPF or UWA application on her PC. As such, you don't need to provide a UI (user interface) that's suited to end-users.

However, for your own use, it could be handy to have an HTML-based UI served by the microservice: that way you can test invoke it using a plain browser, not just an HTTP API client. Sure, we're lazy and not really into providing extra work just to get a handy UI; but what if I told you that Visual Studio can generate it for you just like it did with the API? That's scaffolding again.

5.2 UI scaffolding with Visual Studio

Once again I won't go into details about ASP.NET Core MVC; all you need to known is that handling request that come from a browser require a controller (just like an API), plus a view for each controller action. A view provides the HTML that is displayed inside the user browser.

Visual Studio can scaffold a controller and view that will be enough for basic use. Let me show you.

From the *Solution Explorer* I right-click the *Controllers* folder and select *Add / Controller...* from the contextual menu. In the *Add Scaffold* dialog box I select *MVC Controller with views, using Entity Framework* and click the *Add* button.

An *Add MVC Controller with views, using Entity Framework* dialog box opens. I select *Car* as the *Model class* and *GarageFactory* as the *Data context class*, *CarsUIController* as the controller one and click the *Add* button.

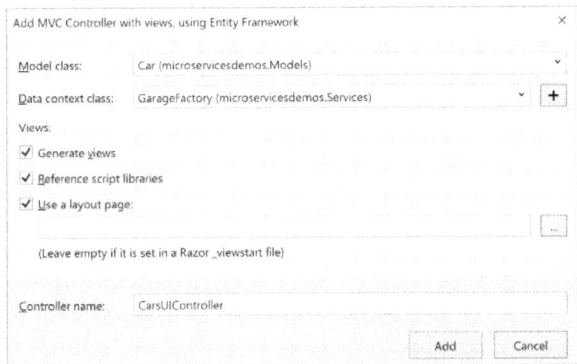

Apart from the *CarsUIController* class, views are created inside the *Views/CarsUI* folder. When I run the application and point my browser to *http://<server>/CarsUI* I get an in-browser list of the rows inside the *cars* table:

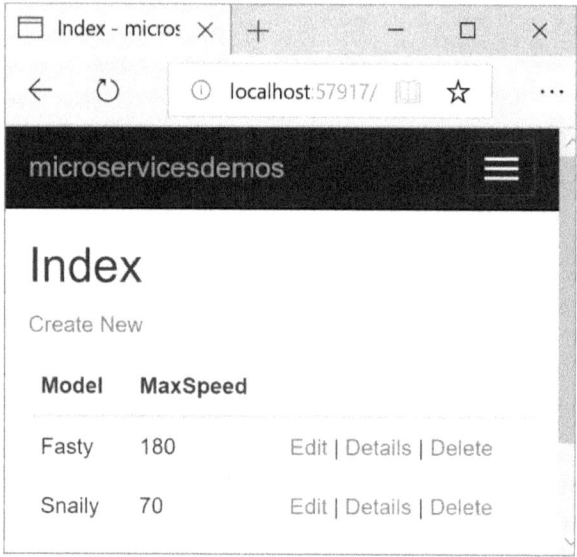

From there I can manage the entries in the table and create new ones. That UI will be published together with my microservice.

5.3 Exercise - Add a UI to the train scheduling service

 Add a HTML user interface to the *ScheduleService* microservice so that a user can browse and create schedules using her browser. That way, both the API and HTML interface will be available.

Change the default values for routing in the *Startup* class so that the *TrainSchedulesViews* controller is used by default instead of the *Home* controller.

Here is what you should get:

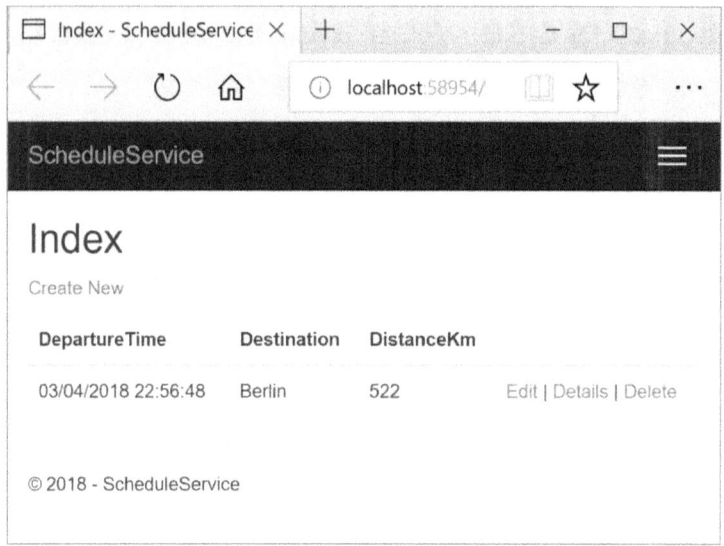

5.4 Exercise solution

- In the *Solution Explorer*, right-click the *Controllers* directory, and select *Add / Controller...* from the context menu.
- In the *Add Scaffold* dialog box, select the *MVC Controller with views, using Entity Framework* template. Click the *Add* button.
- In the *Add API Controller with actions, using Entity Framework* dialog box, enter the following values:
  - Model class: TrainSchedule (ScheduleService.Models)
  - Data context class: TrainsDbContext (ScheduleService.Data)

– Controller name: TrainSchedulesViewsController
- Click the *Add* button.
- Open the *Startup.cs* file and locate the following code:

```
app.UseMvc(routes =>
{
  routes.MapRoute(
    name: "default",
    template: "{controller=Home}/{action=Index}/{id?}");
});
```

- Replace it with the following code:

```
app.UseMvc(routes =>
{
  routes.MapRoute(
    name: "default",
    template: "{controller=TrainSchedulesViews}/{action\
=Index}/{id?}");
});
```

- From the *Debug* menu click *Start Without Debugging*
- Make sure that you can create and edit some schedules using that HTML interface.
- From a PowerShell command-line, type the following command:

```
(Invoke-WebRequest http://localhost:51426/api/TrainSche\
dules).Content
```

- Make sure that the results returned contains the schedules you just created and edited using the HTML interface.

6. Invoking a service from .NET and .NET Core

6.1 .NET Clients

Now that we created the *ScheduleService* microservice, it can be consumed from any client using HTTP. That means virtually any client: servers, smartphones, desktops, or other services.

Since we're coding using .NET Core, chances are that there will be .NET (WPF, ASP.NET) or .NET Core (UWA, ASP.NET Core) clients. In the .NET and .NET Core world, we can use the following classes in order to use microservice APIs that use JSON over HTTP:

- System.Net.Http.HttpClient in order to make HTTP requests and handle responses;
- Newtonsoft.Json.JsonConvert in order to convert JSON to and from .NET objects.

Actually it's easy. Let me show you.

6.2 Demo: consume the microservice from a WPF client

Let's create a plain .NET WPF application that consumes the *ScheduleService* microservice.

We'll keep it simple: we just want to list train schedules.

> The code for this demonstration application is part of the exercises solution. Look at the *Source code* chapter for more information.

First, I'm going to create a new WPF application. I create a brand new Visual Studio solution for that matter since I want to show how separate from the microservice that application can be. In fact, the only link between that WPF application and the scheduling microservice is a URL.

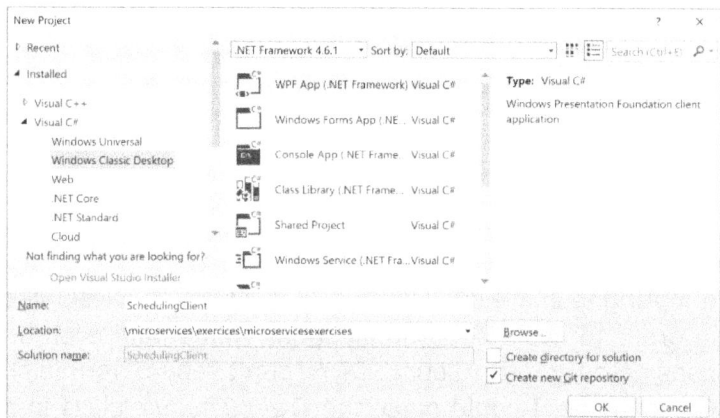

I'll keep the user interface to something very basic: a DataGrid lists the schedules, and a button next to it allows users to refresh its contents. I'm also keeping my XAML as simple as possible:

```
<Window x:Class="SchedulingClient.MainWindow"
    ...>
    <DockPanel>
        <Button Click-"refresh_Click"
                DockPanel.Dock="Bottom"
                Content="Refresh" />
        <DataGrid x:Name="scheduleList" />
    </DockPanel>
</Window>
```

This is a basic application so I'm going to use plain code-behind, not MVVM. If you need to learn MVVM, head for my Learn WPF MVVM[a] book.

[a]https://leanpub.com/learnwpf

Time to add some code. I need a class that represents each train schedule that is received from the API. It's very tempting to share code with the *ScheduleService* service in order to avoid code duplication. That would even be considered good practice: DRY (don't repeat yourself). For instance, I could place the *TrainSchedule* class in a class library that would be referenced from the *ScheduleService* project and the *SchedulingClient* project.

However attracting code reuse may seem for that model class, I strongly advise you not to do so. One of the main reasons for selecting a microservice architecture is decoupling: making sure each part of the application can evolve differently. Code reuse between the projects goes against that: any change in the model, and both the client and server would be impacted. That would be a different story if you version the model classes (using different namespaces for instance); but I'm heading for a simple solution in this demo, so I'm simply going to write another *TrainSchedule* class in the *SchedulingClient* project. In order to show it's not the same, I'm even going to change its name. Hence I'm adding the following class to my *SchedulingClient* project:

```
public class ScheduleItem
{
  public Guid ID { get; set; }
  public DateTime DepartureTime { get; set; }
  public string Destination { get; set; }
  public int DistanceKm { get; set; }
}
```

Next I'm going to write a proxy class that wraps API calls. That proxy class is going to receive JSON and deserialize it. The *Newtonsoft.Json* library is a neat way to (de)serialize JSON to .NET objects, so I add a reference to the *Newtonsoft.Json* NuGet package. I can now code my proxy class:

```
using Newtonsoft.Json;
using System.Collections.Generic;
using System.Net.Http;
using System.Threading.Tasks;

namespace SchedulingClient
{
  public class ScheduleApiProxy
  {
    const string baseUrl = "http://localhost:51426/api";

    public async Task<IEnumerable<ScheduleItem>> GetAll\
Async()
    {
      var url = $"{baseUrl}/TrainSchedules";
```

```
    var client = new HttpClient();
    string json = await client.GetStringAsync(url);
    return JsonConvert.DeserializeObject<IEnumerable<\
ScheduleItem>>(json);
    }
  }
}
```

> In case asynchronous code is new to you, don't
> worry. That's just some nifty syntactic sugar that
> allows for a simple asynchronous code. It's so nifty
> that you can read the code and pretend that the
> *async*, *await* and *Task<>* keywords are not there.

Time to use my proxy class. I write the following code-behind for the XAML UI I created earlier:

```
public partial class MainWindow : Window
{
  public MainWindow()
  {
      InitializeComponent();
  }

  private async void refresh_Click(
    object sender, RoutedEventArgs e)
  {
      var proxy = new ScheduleApiProxy();
```

```
        scheduleList.ItemsSource =
            await proxy.GetAllAsync();
    }
}
```

Here's the result of running my application and clicking its "Refresh" button:

ID	DepartureTime	Destination	DistanceKm
7e61b45e-9a41-4c2d-beb4-0fd0e84dc5f4	4/3/2018 10:56:48 PM	Berlin	522
c291fe26-186d-4390-95de-40a4bfea6c91	4/4/2018 3:05:00 PM	Madrid	832

MainWindow — □ ×

Refresh

7. Invoking a service from another service

7.1 Same but different but same

Remember that schema from the introduction?

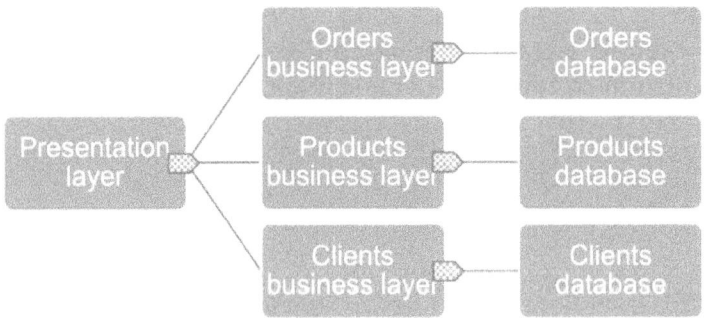

It shows how microservices are connected to each other in a microservice architecture. Each link represents the ability for a microservice to call another. So how do we go on about those calls?

Actually, you already know the answer. In the previous chapter we called a microservice from .NET code. Just use the same code in a microservice itself, and it becomes the client of another microservice. In the schema above I added blocks that show where the .NET client code lies.

7.2 Exercise - Create a ticketing service

Up to now you created a single microservice connected to an in-memory database. You're going to create another independent microservice, then connect the two together. Your scheduling service manages train schedules; in order to manage reservations for the trains you're going to create a ticketing service. Since a ticket is linked to a train schedule, the ticketing service will be consuming the scheduling service.

Create a new microservice named *TicketService*. It should be able to store the following information using an in-memory Entity Framework data context:

- name of the passenger
- ID of the train (a Guid that references a schedule from the *ScheduleService* microservice)

Note that you do not need to make sure that the Guid references an existing train from the *ScheduleService* microservice.

The *TicketService* microservice should expose an API for full CRUD operations and an HTML interface like the *ScheduleService* microservice.

7.3 Exercise solution

- Click on the *File / New / Project...* menu entry.
- In the *New Project* dialog box, select the *ASP.NET Core Web Application* template making sure that you select *Templates / Visual C# / .NET Core* on the left-hand side. In the *Name* zone at the bottom, type "TicketService". On the *Solution* field, select *Create new solution*. Click the *OK* button.
- In the *New ASP.NET Core Web Application* dialog box, select the *.NET Core* and *ASP.NET Core 2.0* at

the top. Select the *Web Application (Model-View-Controler)* template in the middle. Make sure the *Enable Docker Support* checkbox is unchecked. Click the *OK* button.

* Open the *Solution Explorer* clicking on the *View / Solution Explorer* menu entry.
* In the *Solution Explorer*, right-click the *Models* directory, and select *Add / Class...* from the context menu.
* In the *Add New Item* dialog box, type *TrainTicket* in the *Name* field. Click the *Add* button.
* Locate the following code:

```
public class TrainTicket
{
}
```

* Replace it with the following code:

```
public class TrainTicket
{
  public Guid ID { get; set; }
  public string PassengerName { get; set; }

  public Guid TrainScheduleID { get; set; }
}
```

- In the *Solution Explorer*, right-click the *TicketService* project (not the solution) and select *Add / New folder*. Rename the created folder to *Services*.
- In the *Solution Explorer*, right-click the *Services* folder, and select *Add / Class...* from the context menu.
- In the *Add New Item* dialog box, type *TicketsDbContext* in the *Name* field. Click the *Add* button.
- Add the following code at the top of the file:

```
using Microsoft.EntityFrameworkCore;
using TicketService.Models;
```

- Locate the following code:

```
public class TicketsDbContext
{
}
```

- Replace it with the following code:

```
public class TicketsDbContext : DbContext
{
  public TicketsDbContext(
      DbContextOptions<TicketsDbContext> options
  ) : base(options) { }

  public DbSet<TrainTicket> Tickets { get; set; }
}
```

- Open the *Startup.cs* file and add the following code
  to the top of the file:

```
using Microsoft.EntityFrameworkCore;
using TicketService.Services;
```

- In the *Startup* class, add the following code to the
  top of the *ConfigureServices* method:

```
services.AddDbContext<TicketsDbContext>(options =>
    options.UseInMemoryDatabase("trains"));
```

- From the *Build* menu click *Build Solution*
- In the *Solution Explorer*, right-click the *Controllers*
  directory, and select *Add / Controller...* from the
  context menu.

- In the *Add Scaffold* dialog box, select the *API Controller with actions, using Entity Framework* template. Click the *Add* button.
- In the *Add API Controller with actions, using Entity Framework* dialog box, enter the following values:
  - Model class: TrainTicket (TicketService.Models)
  - Data context class: TicketsDbContext (TicketService.Services)
  - Controller name: TrainTicketsController
- Click the *Add* button.
- In the *Solution Explorer*, right-click the *Controllers* directory, and select *Add / Controller...* from the context menu.
- In the *Add Scaffold* dialog box, select the *MVC Controller with views, using Entity Framework* template. Click the *Add* button.
- In the *Add API Controller with actions, using Entity Framework* dialog box, enter the following values:
  - Model class: TrainTicket (TicketService.Models)
  - Data context class: TicketsDbContext (TicketService.Services)
  - Controller name: TrainTicketsViewsController
- Click the *Add* button.
- Open the *Startup.cs* file and locate the following code:

```
app.UseMvc(routes =>
{
  routes.MapRoute(
    name: "default",
    template: "{controller=Home}/{action=Index}/{id?}");
});
```

- Replace it with the following code:

```
app.UseMvc(routes =>
{
  routes.MapRoute(
    name: "default",
    template: "{controller=TrainTicketsViews}/{action=I\
ndex}/{id?}");
});
```

- From the *Debug* menu click *Start Without Debugging*
- Make sure that you can create and edit some tickets using the HTML interface.
- From a PowerShell command-line, type the following command:

```
(Invoke-WebRequest http://localhost:56667/api/TrainTick\
ets).Content
```

- Make sure that the results returned contains the tickets you just created and edited using the HTML interface.

7.4 Exercise - Consume the scheduling service from the ticketing service

 Add a new API to the *TicketService* microservice. It should enable a user to query for a ticket and get full details about the corresponding schedule, plus pricing.

You should handle the following URL:

GET api/TrainTickets/{id}/details

Make sure that you return the following details for the queried ticket:

- passenger name
- train destination
- train departure time
- price (compute it by multiplying the distance by 0.6)

Once you are done, follow on to the Integration testing of the microservices created chapter.

7.5 Exercise solution

- Make sure you are working on the *TicketService* project.
- In the *Solution Explorer*, right-click the *Models* directory, and select *Add / Class...* from the context menu.
- In the *Add New Item* dialog box, type *TicketDetails* in the *Name* field. Click the *Add* button.
- Locate the following code:

```
public class TicketDetails
{
}
```

- Replace it with the following code:

```
public class TicketDetails
{
  public Guid ID { get; set; }
  public string PassengerName { get; set; }
  public string Destination { get; set; }
  public DateTime DepartureTime { get; set; }
  public decimal Price { get; set; }
}
```

- In the *Solution Explorer*, right-click the *Models* directory, and select *Add / Class...* from the context menu.
- In the *Add New Item* dialog box, type *ScheduleItem* in the *Name* field. Click the *Add* button.
- Locate the following code:

```
public class ScheduleItem
{
}
```

- Replace it with the following code:

```
public class ScheduleItem
{
  public Guid ID { get; set; }
  public DateTime DepartureTime { get; set; }
  public string Destination { get; set; }
  public int DistanceKm { get; set; }
}
```

- In the *Solution Explorer*, right-click the *Services* folder, and select *Add / Class...* from the context menu.
- In the *Add New Item* dialog box, type *ScheduleApiProxy* in the *Name* field. Click the *Add* button.
- Add the following code at the top of the file:

```
using TicketService.Models;
using Newtonsoft.Json;
using System.Net.Http;
```

- Locate the following code:

```
public class ScheduleApiProxy
{
}
```

- Replace it with the following code:

```
public class ScheduleApiProxy
{
  const string baseUrl = "http://localhost:51426/api";

  public async Task<ScheduleItem> GetDetailsAsync(Guid \
id)
  {
    var url = $"{baseUrl}/TrainSchedules/{id}";

    var client = new HttpClient();
    string json = await client.GetStringAsync(url);
    return JsonConvert.DeserializeObject<ScheduleItem>(\
json);
  }
}
```

> In this solution we use dependency injection in order
> to get an instance of the proxy to the *ScheduleSer-*
> *vice* microservice. There is no obligation to this: we
> just follow the default ASP.NET Core MVC pattern.

- In the *Startup* class, add the following code to the
  bottom of the *ConfigureServices* method:

```
services.AddTransient<ScheduleApiProxy>();
```

- In the *TrainTicketsController* class, add the following method:

```
// GET: api/TrainTickets/5/details
[HttpGet("{id}/details")]
public async Task<IActionResult> GetTrainTicketDetails(
    [FromRoute] Guid id,
    [FromServices] ScheduleApiProxy proxy
)
{
    var trainTicket = await _context.Tickets
        .SingleOrDefaultAsync(m => m.ID == id);

    if (trainTicket == null)
```

```
{
  return NotFound();
}

  var trainSchedule = await proxy.GetDetailsAsync(train\
Ticket.TrainScheduleID);

  if (trainSchedule == null)
  {
    return NotFound();
  }

  var details = new TicketDetails()
  {
    ID = trainTicket.ID,
    PassengerName = trainTicket.PassengerName,
    Destination = trainSchedule.Destination,
    DepartureTime = trainSchedule.DepartureTime,
    Price = trainSchedule.DistanceKm*0.6M
  };

  return Ok(details);
}
```

- From the *Debug* menu click *Start Without Debugging*

7.6 Integration testing of the microservices created

We're there: we have a microservice architecture. Small and naive, but it's there. The two microservices are available independently, and the ticketing microservice aggregates data from the scheduling service.

Time for some manual integration testing: we're going to create a schedule entry, reference it from a ticket entry, and check that the ticketing service can return aggregated details for those entries.

From a PowerShell command-line, type the following command:

```
Invoke-WebRequest -Method POST -Body '{"departureTime":\
"2018-04-05T14:00:00+01:00","distanceKm":518,"destinati\
on":"Amsterdam","id":"047392b3-12c4-43e9-8c9b-a3f3d9752\
f2c"}' -Header @{"Content-Type"="application/json"} htt\
p://localhost:51426/api/TrainSchedules
```

That creates a schedule entry in the scheduling service. Now type the following command:

```
Invoke-WebRequest -Method POST -Body '{"id":"6e3452dc-b\
11f-4806-8379-1b5b77b604cf","passengerName":"Arthur","t\
rainScheduleId":"047392b3-12c4-43e9-8c9b-a3f3d9752f2c"}\
' -Header @{"Content-Type"="application/json"} http://l\
ocalhost:56667/api/TrainTickets
```

That creates a ticket entry in the ticketing service. Time to check for the integration of both service. Type the following command:

```
(Invoke-WebRequest http://localhost:56667/api/TrainTick\
ets/6e3452dc-b11f-4806-8379-1b5b77b604cf/details).Conte\
nt
```

That command yields the following aggregated result:

```
{"id":"6e3452dc-b11f-4806-8379-1b5b77b604cf","passenger\
Name":"Arthur","destination":"Amsterdam","departureTime\
":"2018-04-05T15:00:00+02:00","price":310.8}
```

Great, isn't it?

I need you, super-hero !

Thank you so much for reading this book. I do hope that it helps you understand and get confident with Microservices, ASP.NET Core and Docker.

As a reader, you are kind of a super-hero: you gain the power to create beautiful and well architectured applications using Microservices and make computers more useful.

Guess what? You have another superpower: to rate this book on the site where you purchased it, or Amazon. You may feel it's nothing, but it is super important for auto-edited books like this one. Please, take some minutes of your precious time to rate this book. That counts a lot for independent authors like myself!

8. Introduction to containers and Docker

8.1 Why do we need containers?

Let's go through some real-world problems. We'll detail in chapter How containers solve problems why containers solve those problems.

The deployment hassle

As a developer, you may be used to suffering when deployment time comes. You surely know that "It works on my machine" expression. You probably used it. Sure the application works on your machine, but the deployment machines are not your coding box. When it comes to deploying the application it may - and will - behave differently.

Your deployment machines don't have the SDK installed. They may not have IIS or other supporting software. They may sport a different OS. They may be hosted servers in the cloud over which you have little control and access. They may even not have a persistent storage.

In short, that lovely environment you have on your machine is most likely not to be present on the deployment machine. That's just part of the trouble, and that's something containers solve.

Continuous integration

Your team probably has a continuous integration and delivery (CI/CD) server somewhere in-house or even in the Cloud. That's good practice since it ensures that your software can be built no matter who changes the source code. Plus it can ensure code quality through static analysis, unit testing, and even deliver your code. That's for the good part.

Now, you know that managing a CI server over time is a tedious task since the server ends up having many build frameworks installed (or references to runner machines that themselves have the build frameworks and need to be maintained). Also, if you ever moved your software builds from one CI system to another (e.g. Jenkins to GitLab), you know that you had to reconfigure the system using yet another way to describe how the software should be built.

I bet you have better things to do in your life. What if you could configure the build system once and for all, test it on your machine then use the same build system on whatever CI server? That's another benefit of containers.

Upgrading common dependencies

As of writing one of my clients has a server hosting several PHP applications and needs to upgrade PHP itself. Since all the applications on the server depend on the PHP version installed they plan to have a hard time doing so, since they cannot update one application at a time. But guess what? We're going to use containers to run their applications, and that will solve the problem: such isolation will allow us to upgrade one application at a time, even if they are hosted on the same server.

DevOps

You either heard about that DevOps trend, or were asked to go DevOps. What is it about? Smart people realized that Devs (you) and Ops (the IT pros, sysadmins, network engineers) have conflicting objectives. Devs want to release software quickly and update them often (you know you want, especially since you have that CI/CD server), while Ops want to ensure system stablllty. DevOps is about removing the conflict that arises from those objectives using processes and tools. And yes, yet again, containers as a tool help solve the DevOps antagonism.

8.2 Virtualization could have been the panacea

As far as the above problems are concerned, a solution has already been tested: virtualization. With virtualization, an actual computer (its OS, software, files) becomes a virtual machine that can be ran across different physical servers, and servers can run several virtual machines. That provides excellent isolation, but it has a tremendous cost: virtual images are fat, they represent huge files and huge amounts of memory are needed to run them.

8.3 Why containers perform better

Containers come from that simple idea: virtualization is great, but it's crazy to virtualize everything. Since many parts of the OS are common to the virtual machines, they can be taken away from the virtual machines and run as common resources while maintaining independence on the surface. That's how containers were born: a container runs isolated from other containers, but it shares actual OS resources with them.

Also, virtual disks share common grounds, so we can avoid duplication. Container images are what describe containers, and each image can be based on an existing image. That way, once a system already has a base image it doesn't need to be uploaded to the system again.

Images can even be shared through common servers, which are called image Registries.

8.4 Containers in practice

Containers

Imagine you want to run one of your microservices. You get a brand new server machine, install the OS and software machine, copy the needed files, configure network connectivity, and run the microservice. Once you're done with the microservice you just trash the server completely. Should you need load-balancing, you can repeat the process in order to have extra servers.

Sure, that sounds too heavy a process, because in real life this process is expensive and time consuming. But that's basically what containers offer. Without the cost or time. Just think of containers as inexpensive fully configured computers that you can grab, use, then dispose of.

Some vocabulary: containers and images

Containers are like running machines. When you create a container, you use a template which is called an *image*. Among other things, an image states which OS is used, which programs are installed, which command is ran when a container using that image is started, which environment variables it uses by default. For any given image, many containers can be ran.

Think of images and containers as equivalents to classes and instances in object-oriented programming: a **class** defines how an **instance** will behave, and there will be many **instances** created from a **class**. That's exactly the same for containers and images: an **image** defines how a **container** will behave, and there will be many **containers** created from an **image**.

In short:

Docker	OOP[1]
Image	Class
Container	Instance

Running a simple image

Let me show you. I have Docker installed and running on my machine, and I want to run a small console application. I open a PowerShell command-line and type:

```
docker run docker/whalesay
```

> In case you receive an error doing so, that may mean you didn't start Docker.

The above instruction asks Docker to run a container based on the *docker/whalesay* image. On first run, Docker downloads the *docker/whalesay* image since it is not present on my system. That image is based on Linux and has a console program called *cowsay* that just echoes a message. However, nothing is displayed since I didn't ask the container to run the *cowsay* program.

Let's instruct Docker to run a new container and make it run the *cowsay* program:

```
docker run docker/whalesay cowsay
```

Now the *cowsay* program is ran and outputs its text to the console:

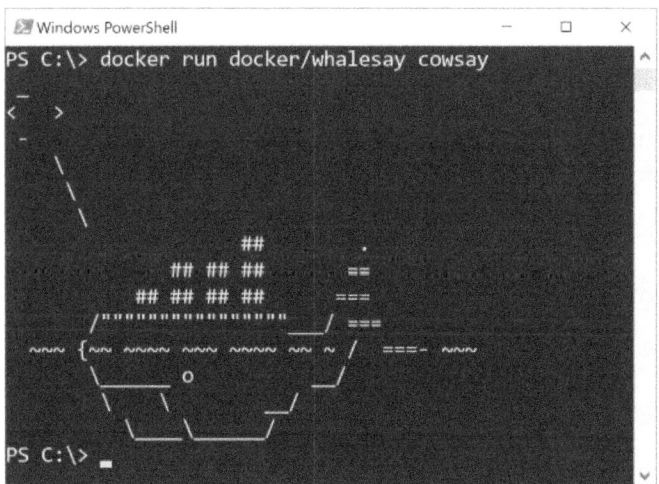

Let's run a container once again, this time passing command-line arguments to the *cowsay* program (the text it needs to echo):

```
docker run docker/whalesay cowsay Microservices rule!
```

We get the same output, however our text has been echoed.

You may not be impressed, but I'd like to underline the fact that during each of the three *docker run* commands above a new container has been created, has executed our instructions, and has been discarded. It may seem like overkill, but you'll grow to love that use-and-discard method because it's efficient and it allows for isolation.

Let's inspect the containers created using the docker ps command:

```
docker ps
```

That command lists the containers running on my system. Right now it returns an empty list. That's normal: the container ran and it did output text to the console, but it has now been terminated. I can list all containers including terminated ones with the following command:

```
docker ps -a
```

I can now see the container that ran the *cowsay* command using the *docker/whalesay* image. The output I get is something along those lines:

CONTAINER ID	IMAGE	STATUS
74532d3d6cff	docker/whalesay	Exited (0)

Note the container ID. It allows us to inspect the defunct container and act over it. Suppose the container was ran in the background, I could get its output using the following command:

```
docker logs 74532d3d6cff
```

And I can completely delete the container using the following command:

```
docker rm 74532d3d6cff
```

In case you wan to run a very short-lived container like the one we just ran, but you don't want to manually delete the container afterwards, you can add the *rm* modifier to the *docker run* command. That way the container will be removed as soon as it ends its processing: no cleanup to do, but you can't access its post-mortem logs. Here's the *docker run* command that includes container cleanup:

```
docker run --rm docker/whalesay cowsay Clean me!
```

Running a server image

The containers we ran above were short lived. But we can run containers that remain alive and serve incoming HTTP requests. In fact, as long as a container's command doesn't exit, the container will keep running.

Also, the *docker run* command allows for a *restart* modifier that enables us to state what action should be taken
whenever the container stops. For instance, if we use
a *restart unless-stopped* modifier the container will be
restarted automatically whether it crashes or the server
is restarted. For instance, the following command would
make for a stable service:

```
docker run --rm nginx
```

NGINX is a server software that can act as a reverse-
proxy, file server or many other things. It's a com-
petitor for IIS.

There's one problem with the *docker run* command used
above for *NGINX* however: it listens on port 80 but
containers are isolated so actually no incoming request
will be routed to the container. The *p* modifier is used
for that matter. It allows us to listen on a physical port
on the hosting machine and route incoming requests to a
port inside the container. Since *NGINX* listens on port 80,
the following command would route incoming requests
on port 8086 to the NGINX instance running inside a
container:

```
docker run -p 8086:80 nginx
```

I can now open a browser and see my NGINX instance
running:

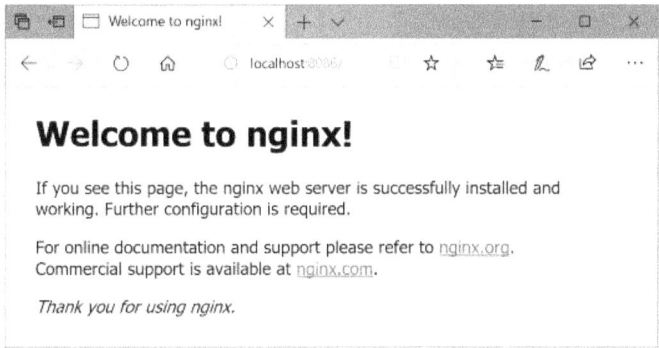

The PowerShell command-line is connected to the running container. I can see console output from NGINX, and my keystrokes are sent to the running container. Should I want my command-line back, I can press *Ctrl-C*. Now I can type commands again. Let's see which containers are running:

```
docker ps
```

We get the following output:

CONTAINER ID	IMAGE	STATUS
b46de8a7ddc3	nginx	Up 5 minutes

Which means the container is still running. Once I'm done with it, I can explicitly stop the container, then remove its dead body:

```
docker stop b46de8a7ddc3
docker rm b46de8a7ddc3
```

Did you like that? Server software without any installation, right? Let's run two more containers:

```
docker run -p 8087:80 wordpress:4.9.4-php5.6-apache
docker run -p 8088:80 epod/schedule
```

The first one is the famous Wordpress CMS, and the second one is the microservice you created in the *Microservices server-side* chapter. Note you can run those commands on your machine and seamlessly get the same programs running in a breeze. When the images aren't present on your machine already, Docker downloads them from a registry (more about that later).

Here's what I get when I point my browser to those running containers:

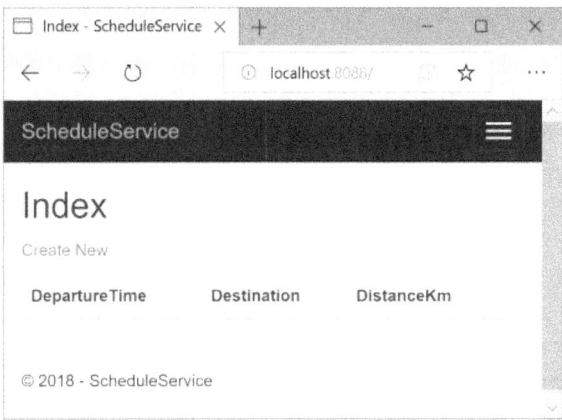

That should be the *wow!* moment where you realize how containers are going to simplify your deployments. We just ran the microservice I created in a breeze. No OS, runtime or software install: you get everything from a single *docker run* command, without any surprise.

8.5 How containers solve problems

As such, containers offer solutions to the problems I mentioned previously:

- The deployment hassle: a container is fully described as an image. That image contains everything (OS, platform software, files) so it runs exactly the same on your machine and any server.
- Continuous integration: not only can you ship your software as images, you can also build and test its

artifacts inside containers. That ensures your build
and tests are described once whatever the CI system that runs them, and that they are independent
from one software to another.

- Upgrading common dependencies: images contain
  platform software. When you upgrade the platform
  software in an image, you don't alter other images.
- DevOps: instead of shipping files and procedures,
  developer ship container images for whatever software they produce. Ops just need to offer a platform for running and orchestrating containers from
  those images, whatever the actual software platform.

8.6 Containers as microservice hosts

Let's face it: a microservice architecture makes deployment complex. Each microservice is one more application
to deploy. They may be deployed on a common machine
or different machines, on a Cloud or on-premises server.
Since services are loosely coupled they can each use a
different platform (.NET Core, Node.JS, PHP, …). Plus
each service may be load-balanced. As such, deploying
microservices could quickly become a nightmare.

Except now we have the right tooling: we saw that containers allow deploying server programs as container in a
breeze, no matter the platform used inside the container.
Sure you can deploy your microservices ignoring the

container technology, but you're going to have a hard time.

8.7 Exercise - Run a Docker container

 Run the *hello-world* Docker image as a container on your machine.

Check that the corresponding container appears in the list of terminated containers.

8.8 Exercise solution

- Make sure Docker is running: its icon should be displayed in your taskbar. Otherwise start it from the Start menu.
- From a PowerShell command-line, type the following command:

```
docker run --rm hello-world
```

- Check that an informational message is displayed.
- From a PowerShell command-line, type the following command:

```
docker ps -a
```

- Check that a container using the *hello-world* image appears as "Exited" in the displayed list.

9. Creating and running Docker images

9.1 How images are built

Now that you learnt how to run containers based on existing images, it's high time you learned how to package your microservices as images. This will enable your microservices to benefit from all the features containers bring.

Creating your own Docker images is fairly simple. Actually, you need to describe in a file how the image is created, then invoke the *docker build* command. The file should be called *Dockerfile* if you want to use defaults.

Remember the *docker/whalesay* image we used in the previous chapter? When running a container based on it, we need to explicitly invoke the *cowsay* executable and provide it with a text to output:

```
docker run --rm docker/whalesay cowsay Clean me!
```

How about we simplified that? I want to to create an image that invokes the *cowsay* executable by default. For this, I create a file named *Dockerfile* with the following content:

```
FROM docker/whalesay
ENTRYPOINT ["cowsay", "Microservices rule!"]
```

The *FROM* instruction tells Docker what other image your image should be based on. It could be a basic Linux image, but you are free to use whatever other image according to your needs. In our case we could start from a plain Linux image and install the *cowsay* executable, but why bother? I'm simply basing my image on the *docker/whalesay* image that already contains the *cowsay* executable.

Next comes an *ENTRYPOINT* instruction, that states which command should be ran when the container starts. That's about all I need, here. In case you wonder, a full list of *Dockerfile* instructions can be found here[1].

Next we need to invoke the *docker build* command that will create an image from *Dockerfile* instructions. *docker build* expects the image name, called a *tag* (using the *t* modifier) and the directory that will be used as the build context. We'll see more about that later, but for the moment it's the directory where the *Dockerfile* is located.

I'm going to open a PowerShell command-line, set the current directory to the one where my *Dockerfile* file is located, and run the following command:

```
docker build -t simplesay .
```

Note that there is a dot at the end of the *docker build* instruction. What we tell Docker is that the image tag

---

[1] https://docs.docker.com/engine/reference/builder/

should be *simplesay* and that it should use the current directory (hence the dot) as the build context.

Here is the output I get:

```
Sending build context to Docker daemon  2.048kB
Step 1/2 : FROM docker/whalesay
 ---> 6b362a9f73eb
Step 2/2 : ENTRYPOINT ["cowsay", "Microservices rule!"]
 ---> Running in 29d0d52a8453
Removing intermediate container 29d0d52a8453
 ---> 33ec79c60b01
Successfully built 33ec79c60b01
Successfully tagged simplesay:latest
```

It confirms that the image was built and tagged as *simplesay:latest*. We can check the available images on my machine by running the *docker image list* command. My *simplesay* image appears along with any other image that was previously downloaded. Here's an extract of the output I get:

REPOSITORY	TAG	CREATED
simplesay	latest	2 minutes ago
nginx	latest	7 weeks ago

Note that the *latest* tag was added to the image name I provided. In fact a full tag takes the following form:

```
repository/name:version
```

We'll talk about the *repository* part later on. The version part is supposed to be *latest* when missing. That means any new image you build with will replace the previous one. It's good practice to use version numbers when tagging the images you release, so that containers can be ran with the exact version needed (especially great for rolling back to previous versions in case a new deployment is problematic). For now, I want to keep things simple so I'll omit the version, which means my image will always be the *latest* one.

Now that I created an image, I can run it:

```
docker run simplesay
```

That's it: my image outputs text without any need to provide it any parameter. It's so great I'd love to publish it and that's what we'll see in the next chapter. For now, let's just realize that publishing such a simple image isn't going to change the world, so I'd better aim for a nicer image. How about publishing an ASP.NET Core microservice as an image?

9.2 An ASP.NET Core Dockerfile

Visual Studio can generate the *Dockerfile* for us, but if you look at it you may find it complex. I'd like you to

> actually *understand* what we're doing so we're going to create the *Dockerfile* manually.

Alright, let's publish an ASP.NET Core microservice as an image so that many containers can be spawn from it. That means creating a *Dockerfile*, which in turn means answering the following question: what does an ASP.NET Core microservice needs in order to be ran?

1. The service should be compiled into a DLL and its dependencies.
2. The .NET Core runtime should be installed.
3. The DLL and dependencies should be present as files.
4. The microservice listens on port 80.
5. For the microservice to listen, it needs to be started using the *dotnet* executable.

The first point is obtained by using the *Publish* command from Visual Studio. The next ones can be described in a *Dockerfile*.

When I invoke the *docker build* command, it runs the *Dockerfile* instructions and accesses the files present in the *Dockerfile* directory. As such, I want my *Dockerfile* to be present in the root of the publication directory where the application will be built; hence I'm going to place it at the root of my project and require that Visual Studio copies it to the output directory.

Remember the *microservicesdemo* project that I created earlier? I want to publish that one. In the *Solution Explorer* I'm going to right-click the project name and select *Add / New Item...* from the contextual menu. In the *Add New Item* dialog box I select *Text file* and name it *Dockerfile*, then click the *Add* button.

Visual Studio is quite stubborn and names the file *Dockerfile.txt*, so I rename it to *Dockerfile* with no extension. I then add the following content to the *Dockerfile* file:

```
FROM microsoft/aspnetcore:2.0
WORKDIR /app
COPY . .
EXPOSE 80
ENTRYPOINT ["dotnet", "microservicesdemos.dll"]
```

The first line states that the base image is based on an image that contains the .NET Core runtime (more details here[2])

The *WORKDIR* instruction states that the following commands will act on files that are located in the */app* directory of the image being built.

The *COPY* instruction takes all the files that are present in the context directory (the one where my *Dockerfile* file lives) and copies them in the */app* directory of the image.

The *EXPOSE* instruction specifies that this image listens on port 80.

---

[2]https://hub.docker.com/r/microsoft/aspnetcore/

The *ENTRYPOINT* instruction states that when a container is spawn using my image it will execute the following command:

```
dotnet microservicesdemos.dll
```

Which is great, because it runs my ASP.NET Core microservice.

In order to make sure the *Dockerfile* is present in the build directory, I right-click it in the Solution Explorer and select *Properties* in the contextual menu. I set the following two properties:

- Build Action: **Content**
- Copy to Output Directory: **Copy if newer**

Time for Visual Studio to build my application. In the Solution Explorer I right-click the *Publish...* entry. In the main *Publish* pane, I click the *Folder* icon (you may need to scroll to the right), keep the proposed folder then click the *Publish* button:

Once publishing is done, I open the publish directory in a PowerShell command line and build my image:

```
cd bin
cd Release
cd PublishOutput
docker build -t msdemos .
```

And that's it! My image is ready. Now let's spawn a new container running that image. Note the use of the *p* argument so that port 80 of the container is bound to a physical port on my machine:

```
docker run --rm -p 8091:80 msdemos
```

Here's the output of the *docker run* command. It's the actual console output of my microservice:

```
warn: Microsoft.AspNetCore.DataProtection.KeyManagement\
.XmlKeyManager[35]
      No XML encryptor configured. Key {551c414f-9caf-4\
df9-8a49-bfaf2776ce5b} may be persisted to storage in u\
nencrypted form.
Hosting environment: Production
Content root path: /app
Now listening on: http://[::]:80
Application started. Press Ctrl+C to shut down.
```

I can now point my browser to the following URL:

`http://localhost:8091`

Note that I can run the *docker run* command again and again, using different ports, and I'll have different, isolated, instances of my application listening on those ports.

Let's not forget to stop the container once we're done. The *docker ps* command gives me the container ID.

`docker stop 8d1a66167822`

9.3 Multi-stage Dockerfiles

We learnt enough for you to create an ASP.NET Core image. Later on, however, you may want to go further.

Currently you need to *publish* your application using Visual Studio (the .NET Core SDK, in fact) before it is ready to be ran in an image based on the runtime. We can do better and build and publish your application inside a Docker image.

Why would we want to do so? First for automation purposes. But really, the reason why you want to do so is that you can then build and publish your code on whatever machine has Docker installed: no need for Visual Studio or the .NET Core SDK installed. Yes: that means you can build and create your image on your machine, on a CI/CD system (GitLab, Jenkins) or even in the Cloud.

How many time did you fight with a code base in order to build it? How much time does it take you to configure a CI system for your application? Forget about that. The only dependency you'll need is Docker.

We could add build and publish instructions to our Dockerfile but that wouldn't actually work: our base image contains the .NET Core runtime only. We could use a base image that contains the SDK (*microsoft/aspnet-core-build*), but that image weights 2 GB while the runtime-only image weights 0.3 GB. Why ship an image that contains the whole SDK when all you want to ship is a microservice?

There's a better way. Remember my allegory about using computers and trashing them? We can do that. We can run a container based on the full SDK image, make it build and publish the application, get the files that were published, then trash that container and use the published files inside another image that's based on the runtime only. That could mean using two *Dockerfile* files, but Docker allows us to group all of this in a single *Dockerfile* file. It's called a *multi-stage Dockerfile*.

Visual Studio knows how to generate that file. It creates the appropriate *Dockerfile* if you check the *Enable Docker support* checkmark in the project creation dialog. Or you can add it afterwards by right-clicking the project in the Solution Explorer and selecting *Add / Docker Support* from the contextual menu.

9.4 Exercise - Build and run your own Docker image

 Create a Docker image named *schedule* that hosts your *ScheduleService* microservice you created earlier.

Run the *schedule* image as a container listening on the port 8081 on your machine and check that you can access it using your browser and API calls.

9.5 Exercise solution

- Make sure you are working on the *ScheduleService* project.
- In the *Solution Explorer*, right-click the project (not the solution), and select *Add / New Item...* from the context menu.
- In the *Add New Item* dialog box, select the *Text File* template and type *Dockerfile* in the *Name* field. Click the *Add* button.
- Rename the *Dockerfile.txt* file to *Dockerfile* (no extension).
- Add the following instructions to the *Dockerfile* file:

```
FROM microsoft/aspnetcore:2.0
WORKDIR /app
COPY . .
EXPOSE 80
ENTRYPOINT ["dotnet", "ScheduleService.dll"]
```

- In the *Solution Explorer*, right-click the *Dockerfile* file, and select *Properties* from the context menu and set the following properties:
  - Build action: Content
  - Copy to Output Directory: Copy always
- In the *Solution Explorer*, right-click the project (not the solution), and select *Publish...* from the context menu.
- Select the *Folder* publish option and keep the proposed *binReleasePublishOutput* folder.
- Click the *Publish* button next to the folder name.
- From a PowerShell command-line, change the current directory to *ScheduleService\binReleasePublishOutput*
- Type the following command in the PowerShell command-line:

```
docker build -t schedule .
```

 Don't forget the trailing dot in the above command. It represents the current directory.

- Type the following command in the PowerShell command-line:

```
docker run -d -p 8081:80 schedule
```

- Point your browser to the following URL and check that you get the service HTML interface:

```
http://localhost:8081
```

- From a PowerShell command-line, type the following command:

```
Invoke-WebRequest -Method POST -Body '{"departureTime":\
"2018-04-03T21:56:48.6711219+01:00","distanceKm":1054,"\
destination":"Berlin"}' -Header @{"Content-Type"="appli\
cation/json"} http://localhost:8081/api/TrainSchedules
```

- Refresh your browser and check that you can see the schedule you just added.

> Note that the container keeps running in the background, listening for HTTP requests on port 8081. You can stop it manually.

10. Publishing images to Docker registries

10.1 Why bother with Registries?

In the previous chapter you built an image and ran a container based on that image. You get the power to reliably run as many containers as needed, with reproducible results. The *only* problem - and it is *huge*, is that containers can only be ran from your local machine. Try and run that command on any other computer:

```
docker run -d -p 8081:80 schedule
```

Docker answers that it cannot find the *schedule* image. That command only works on the computer where you ran the image.

This is what registries are for. Registries are image stores. Once an image is built, you can publish it to a Registry. Those who can access the Registry will be able to run your image: when the image is not available locally, Docker tries and pulls it from a Registry. In fact, when you ran the *hello-world* image earlier, it wasn't present on your machine so Docker downloaded it.

This is what an actual workflow could look like:

1. An image is built locally.
2. Optional: a Container is ran locally in order to test the image.
3. The image is published to a Registry.
4. The computer that actually needs to run a container from the image connects to the Registry and downloads the image.

In a simplified way, a DevOps workflow would be:

In a more detailed way, there are three tiers involved: the build machine that creates the image and publishes it, the Registry that hosts the image, the executing machine that fetches the image from the Registry in order to run some containers from that image. Both the build machine and executing machine reference the Registry, and as such they don't need to know each other:

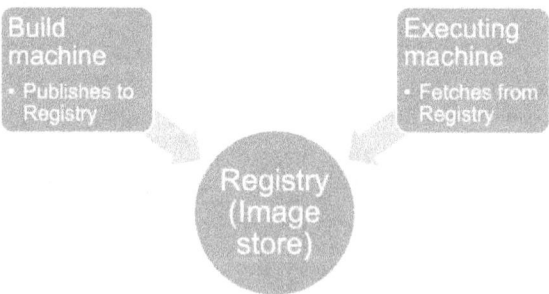

Thanks to registries, we get the realization of the "runs the same everywhere" promise. Once your image runs in a satisfying way on you system, publish it and other computers will run it in the same way.

10.2 Available Registries

A Docker Registry implements a standard API that allow the publisher and consumer to access it. As such, registries are interchangeable.

There are many ways you can get a Docker Registry. Let's see some of them.

Docker Hub

The Docker Hub is a cloud-based (SaaS) registry that's readily available. Just create an account with Docker (a Docker ID) and you're good to go.

You can head on to that page[1] in order to create your Docker ID or browse the Docker Hub.

As of writing, you can publish as many public images as needed on Docker Hub, and one private for free. Paid plans allow you to publish more private images.

---

[1] https://hub.docker.com/

As a container

Should you still doubt that that containers are a useful deployment technology, you can run the Docker Registry as a container. All that it takes is popping a container:

```
docker run -d -p 5000:5000 registry:2
```

It's a little more complicated than that actually. Registries need to be secured with TLS before they can be accessed from outside. Read more information there[2] and more specifically there[3].

> Registries need to be secured because you're actually **storing executable code** there.
>
> What would happen if a man-in-the-middle attack allowed the attacker to add random code to the image you are storing or the one being downloaded? Horrible things, if you ask. Just imagine.
>
> That's why TLS needs to be used in order to deter man-in-the-middle attacks.

---

[2]https://hub.docker.com/_/registry/
[3]https://docs.docker.com/registry/deploying/#run-an-externally-accessible-registry

Azure Container Registry

Who wants to host a registry when it can be cloud-hosted? Azure Container Registry (ACR)[4] allows you to create your own private registry in a breeze.

You may use the Azure Portal or a PowerShell command like the following ones

```
az login
az acr create --resource-group <group> --name <yourname\
> --sku Basic --admin-enabled true
```

> Note that you need to install the Azure CLI in order to issue those commands. It can be installed from there[a].
>
> [a]https://docs.microsoft.com/fr-fr/cli/azure/install-azure-cli?view=azure-cli-latest

And more

There are many other ways to get Docker Registries, and it really depends on what tools you are already using. For instance:

- On AWS, you can host your registry using Amazon Elastic Container Registry (ECR)[5].

[4]https://azure.microsoft.com/services/container-registry/
[5]https://aws.amazon.com/fr/ecr/

- If you are using GitLab, you can activate the GitLab Registry.

10.3 Publishing an image

Publishing an image is a simple process. All you need to do is:

1. Log into the registry
2. Tag your image
3. Push your image to the registry

Let's get into details.

Log into the registry

This step depends on the registry you are using. For the Docker Hub, you can use the *docker login* command. Either you provide it with your login (your Docker ID) information as switches, either it prompts for that information.

The interactive way simply is:

```
docker login
```

Tag your image

As I wrote earlier, a full tag takes the following form:

```
repository/name:version
```

On Docker Hub, the repository part is your Docker ID. Hence when your Docker ID is *yourid*, you need to tag your image with that ID.

The *docker tag* command allows you to add a new tag to an existing image. For instance, if you have an image named *someimage* and want to publish it on Docker Hub, you can first tag it using the following command:

```
docker tag someimage yourid/someimage:latest
```

Now you're ready to push your image to the registry.

Push your image to the registry

This is the final part. It's done using the *docker push* command.

For instance, here's the command that pushes the image created above:

```
docker push yourid/someimage:latest
```

Docker pushes the image in parts to the registry. The caching system it used during the build process is also applied to image pushes. That means Docker will not push image layers that were already published to a registry.

As a result, subsequent pushes of an updated image are faster than the first push. Even the first push is faster when the registry already contains images that use the same base image as the one you're pushing.

10.4 Exercise - Publish your services on Docker Hub

 Publish the *schedule* image on the *Docker Hub* repository.

Create a Docker image named *ticket* that hosts the *TicketService* microservice you created earlier.

Assuming your account name on Docker Hub is *yourname*, your microservices should now be available on Docker Hub as images called *yourname/schedule* and *yourname/ticket*

10.5 Exercise solution

- Create an account on Docker Hub: https://hub.docker.com/
- Type the following command in a PowerShell command-line and log-in using the account you just created:

```
docker login
```

- Type the following commands in the PowerShell command-line (assuming your login is *yourname*):

```
docker tag schedule yourname/schedule:latest
docker push yourname/schedule:latest
```

- Make sure you are working on the *TicketService* project.
- In the *Solution Explorer*, right-click the project (not the solution), and select *Add / New Item…* from the context menu.
- In the *Add New Item* dialog box, select the *Text File* template and type *Dockerfile* in the *Name* field. Click the *Add* button.
- Rename the *Dockerfile.txt* file to *Dockerfile* (no extension).
- Add the following instructions to the *Dockerfile* file:

```
FROM microsoft/aspnetcore:2.0
WORKDIR /app
COPY . .
EXPOSE 80
ENTRYPOINT ["dotnet", "TicketService.dll"]
```

- In the *Solution Explorer*, right-click the *Dockerfile* file, and select *Properties* from the context menu and set the following properties:
  - Build action: Content
  - Copy to Output Directory: Copy always
- In the *Solution Explorer*, right-click the project (not the solution), and select *Publish...* from the context menu.
- Select the *Folder* publish option and keep the proposed *binReleasePublishOutput* folder.
- Click the *Publish* button next to the folder name.
- From a PowerShell command-line, change the current directory to *TicketService\binReleasePublishOutput*
- Type the following command in the PowerShell command-line:

```
docker build -t yourname/ticket:latest .
docker push yourname/ticket:latest
```

 Don't forget the trailing point in the above command. It represents the current directory.

11. Executing linked microservice containers in a Docker Swarm

11.1 The need for orchestrators

Containers are a splendid way to deploy microservices. In fact, deployment of each microservice becomes almost painless.

The trouble is that a microservice-based solution typically involves many microservices. Can you imagine yourself manually deploy and maintain a container for each microservice? If you think that can be painful, just think about what a hell it's going to be when you need to:

- deploy containers across several machines;
- reference each microservice from the ones that call them;
- scale up, which means deploying several containers for each microservice and load-balance between them;

- update all of that;
- ensure things run similarly on your box and deployment servers.

You really don't want that trouble. That's where *orches-trators* come. Orchestrators are like an operating system for containers: they ensure you can meet all of the above goals in a painless way.

11.2 Orchestrators commonly used with Docker

Two orchestrators are commonly used with Docker: *Kubernetes* and *Docker Swarm*.

Which one will you choose? That's up to you. When you install Docker CE on your development machine, you get Swarm included. Kubernetes is also included from version 18.06 upwards.

While Kubernetes has a wider acceptance (it is provided as a managed cloud solution in Azure and AWS for in-stance), it is harder to configure. So I suggest you begin with Swarm, and optionally move to Kubernetes later on.

Most of the concepts are similar between Kubernetes and Swarm, and when using YAML configuration files you should feel at home should you switch from Swarm to Kubernetes. Let's learn Swarm basics.

11.3 Docker Swarm concepts

Docker Swarm spreads your containers (called *tasks*) across several machines (called *nodes*), but you can use it with a single machine. In case there are several nodes, the main one is called the *manager*, and other nodes are called *worker* nodes. You send your commands to the manager.

Here is an example swarm spreading across 3 machines:

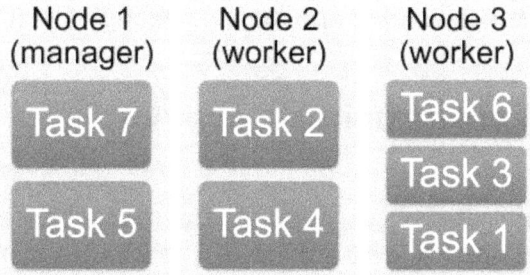

11.4 Creating a swarm

In order to create a swarm on your machine, which becomes the *manager* node of the swarm, you run the following command:

```
docker swarm init
```

That command outputs a token. This token is used when joining worker nodes (that is, other machines) to the swarm. In such a case, you simply need to issue the following command on the other machines, using the token you obtained:

```
docker swarm join --token <token> ip:2377
```

You do not need to have several nodes. A single manager node is enough and allows you to run all of the containers that make up your microservice-based application. So the *docker swarm init* command is enough for now.

11.5 Configuring a stack

Your application is made of several microservices. Each microservice will be a *service* in a *stack* that you create. The stack represents the whole application and allows you to manage the application as a single unit.

Docker Swarm allows you to *describe* the stack and its services in a YAML file. By **describing** what you want instead of stating how to obtain it, Docker Swarm can manage the necessary state changes for you. This is especially great when updating your stack, and is in fact what is called *Infrastructure as code (IaC)*.

> YAML is yet another way to describe objects and arrays of these, just like JSON or XML. It's supposed to be more human-friendly, and you can learn about it there[a].
>
> ---
> [a]http://yaml.org/

The YAML file contains a list of services and the virtual network(s) that those services use to communicate. Suppose we have two services named *first* and *second*. The YAML file simply needs to list the two services:

docker-compose.yml

```
version: "3"
services:
  first:
    image: my/firstimage:1.0
  second:
    image: my/secondimage:1.5
```

Note that the above YAML configuration states which image should be used in order to create the container for each service.

Now suppose that the *first* and *second* services need to communicate with each other. We want a virtual network to be created, and we'll name it *localapi*. Here is how we update the YAML file, and in fact this is the complete version of the YAML file for our stack:

docker-compose.yml

```
version: "3"
services:
  first:
    image: my/firstimage:1.0
    ports:
      - "8181:80"
    networks:
      - localapi
  second:
    image: my/secondimage:1.5
    ports:
      - "8182:80"
    networks:
      - localapi
networks:
  localapi:
```

At the bottom we just listed the virtual network we need, and each service references the network it can access.

Note that I added a *ports* property. That's exactly the same as the *p* switch used in the *docker run* command. We are stating that port 80 exposed by the *my/firstimage:1.0* image will be routed to port 8181 of the hosting machine. That is, the *first* microservice will be available externally on the http://localhost:8181 URL.

One thing I believe is awesome in the way Docker Swarm manages virtual networks is that it provides a DNS server that allows any service to access another one (on the same virtual network) using its name. For instance, if the *second* service needs to invoke the *first* service it can use the following URL: *http://first:80* or, more succinctly: *http://first*. In that case, the internal port (80) exposed by the service is used, whatever the external port on which it is exposed.

11.6 Deploying and managing a stack on a swarm

This is actually the easy part. Just run the following command:

```
docker stack deploy -c docker-compose.yml <stack_name>
```

That will create your stack with the name provided. Plus all of the services and networks required in the YAML file. I told you that was easy, didn't I?

Should you make any change to the YAML file, for example change the version number (tag) of some images used by the services, or add/remove services and networks, you can simply run the exact same *docker stack deploy* command and your stack will be updated to the current contents of the YAML file.

Use the same YAML file on your deployment servers, and you get the same results. Not only is orchestration easy, it actually is extremely powerful.

In case you want to make sure that the services were deployed, or need to list the tasks, you can use the following commands:

```
docker service ls
docker service ps <stack_name>
```

Eventually, when you need to get rid of the stack (on your development machine for instance), use the following command:

```
docker stack rm <stack_name>
```

You can even take your computer back to normal by asking it to leave the swarm:

```
docker swarm leave --force
```

11.7 Exercise - Run the two services in a Docker Swarm

Create a swarm using your local machine.

Configure a stack named *trainservices* where the *schedule* and *ticket* services run and are exposed on ports 8084 and 8085 externally.

Make sure the stack contains an internal network that allows the *ticket* service to call the *schedule* service.

In order to achieve this exercise you need to change the URL used by the *ticket* service in order to call the *schedule* service, and rebuild its image (see first points of the solution).

 Once you are done, follow on to the Integration testing of the stack created chapter.

11.8 Exercise solution

- Open the *ScheduleApiProxy.cs* file of the *Services* directory in the *TicketService* project.
- Locate the following code:

```
const string baseUrl = "http://localhost:51426/api";
```

- Replace it with the following code:

```
const string baseUrl = "http://schedule/api";
```

- In the *Solution Explorer*, right-click the project (not the solution), and select *Publish...* from the context menu.
- Click the *Publish* button from the *Publish* page.
- From a PowerShell command-line, change the current directory to *TicketService\binReleasePublishOutput*
- Type the following commands in the PowerShell command-line:

```
docker build -t yourname/ticket:latest .
docker push yourname/ticket:latest
```

- Create a file named *docker-compose.yml* in any directory.
- Add the following instructions to the *docker-compose.yml* file:

```
version: "3"
services:
  schedule:
    image: yourname/schedule:latest
    ports:
      - "8084:80"
    networks:
      - localapi
  ticket:
    image: yourname/ticket:latest
    ports:
```

```
        - "8085:80"
      networks:
        - localapi
    networks:
      localapi:
```

- From a PowerShell command-line, change the current directory to the directory where you created the *docker-compose.yml* file.
- Type the following commands in the PowerShell command-line:

```
docker swarm init
docker stack deploy -c docker-compose.yml trainservices
```

- Wait for the stack to initialize.
- Point your browser to the following URL:

http://localhost:8084

- Check that you can see a list of empty train schedules.

Our stack runs the services in containers that are isolated from the previous ones, which means the in-memory data of the services manually launched previously isn't available there.

11.9 Integration testing of the stack created

Now we still have a microservice architecture bud there's a huge difference: it's running in a Docker Stack. That stack only runs on our local computer, but it would be almost effortless to make it spread over several machines, whether on-promises or in the Cloud.

We can now repeat our manual integration testing, targeting the services running inside the Docker Stack.

Once again, we're going to create a schedule entry, reference it from a ticket entry, and check that the ticketing service can return aggregated details for those entries.

From a PowerShell command-line, type the following command:

```
Invoke-WebRequest -Method POST -Body '{"departureTime":\
"2018-04-05T14:00:00+01:00","distanceKm":518,"destinati\
on":"Amsterdam","id":"047392b3-12c4-43e9-8c9b-a3f3d9752\
f2c"}' -Header @{"Content-Type"="application/json"} htt\
p://localhost:8084/api/TrainSchedules
```

That creates a schedule entry in the scheduling service. Now type the following command:

```
Invoke-WebRequest -Method POST -Body '{"id":"6e3452dc-b\
11f-4806-8379-1b5b77b604cf","passengerName":"Arthur","t\
rainScheduleId":"047392b3-12c4-43e9-8c9b-a3f3d9752f2c"}\
' -Header @{"Content-Type"="application/json"} http://l\
ocalhost:8085/api/TrainTickets
```

That creates a ticket entry in the ticketing service. Time to check for the integration of both service. Type the following command:

```
(Invoke-WebRequest http://localhost:8085/api/TrainTicke\
ts/6e3452dc-b11f-4806-8379-1b5b77b604cf/details).Conten\
t
```

That command yields the following aggregated result:

```
{"id":"6e3452dc-b11f-4806-8379-1b5b77b604cf","passenger\
Name":"Arthur","destination":"Amsterdam","departureTime\
":"2018-04-05T15:00:00+02:00","price":310.8}
```

Same services, but ready to be deployed as a stack. If you think about it, we're doing DevOps in such a seamless way…

But wait for it: we can do better.

12. Microservice clusters using Docker Swarm

12.1 Demo: load-balancing the stack

How about scaling up our services? Suppose we now have thousands of users that want to use our services, so we need to run each of the services in several containers, spread over several machines in the Cloud? This means load-balancing the HTTP requests to both services and from the ticketing service to the scheduling service. Can we? Yes, and it's simple.

Currently we have two containers. Just to be sure, I type the following command:

```
docker service ps trainservices
```

It yields results that look like:

IMAGE	DESIRED STATE	CURRENT STATE
yourname/ schedule :latest	Running	Running 3 minutes ago
yourname/ ticket :latest	Running	Running 3 minutes ago

Let's add a deploy property to the docker-compose.yml file:

```
version: "3"
services:
  schedule:
    image: yourname/schedule:latest
    ports:
      - "8084:80"
    networks:
      - localapi
    deploy:
      replicas: 3
      resources:
        limits:
          cpus: "0.1"
          memory: 100M
      restart_policy:
        condition: on-failure
  ticket:
    image: yourname/ticket:latest
    ports:
      - "8085:80"
    networks:
```

```
  - localapi
 deploy:
  replicas: 2
networks:
 localapi:
```

In order to tell Docker Stack that it should update and take our new requirements into account, I simply type the same command I used for deployment:

```
docker stack deploy -c docker-compose.yml trainservices
```

This is how simple it gets. Currently we are running 5 containers on our local machine, but they could as well be spread over several machines.

If I try and browse to the http://localhost:8085 URL, I get alternatively those two results:

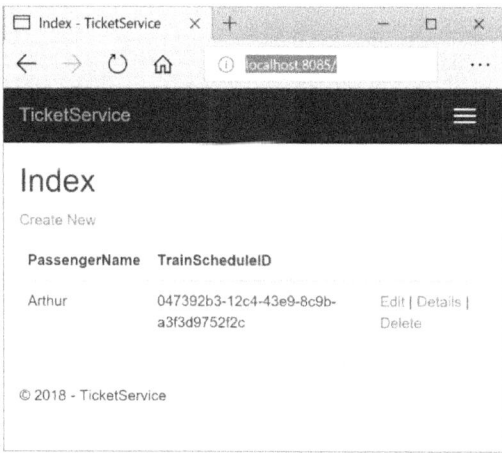

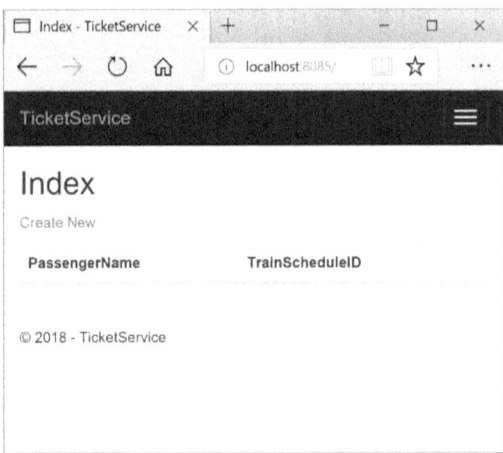

Can you guess why? Yes, there are two replicas of the ticketing service container, and Docker Stack is load-balancing incoming requests to the two containers. If you had told me 10 years ago I could scale up services so seamlessly across machines I'd have laughed. It's just ridiculously simple.

Time for a little cleanup so that we end up with a clean machine: I'm going to take that stack (and its services) and swarm down, using the following commands:

```
docker stack rm trainservices
docker swarm leave --force
```

A word from the author

I sincerely hope you enjoyed reading this book as much as I liked writing it and that you quickly become proficient enough with Microservices, ASP.NET Core and Docker.

If you would like to get in touch you can use :

- email: books@aweil.fr
- Facebook: https://facebook.com/learncollection

In case your project needs it, I'm also available for speaking, teaching, consulting and coding, all around the world.

If you liked this book, you probably saved a lot of time thanks to it. I'd be very grateful if you took some minutes of your precious time to leave a comment on the site where you purchased this book. Thanks a ton!

The Learn collection

This book is part of the *Learn collection*.

The *Learn collection* allows developers to self-teach new technologies in a matter of days.

Published books

- Learn ASP.NET Core MVC[1]
- Learn ASP.NET MVC[2]
- Learn Meteor[3]
- Learn Microservices[4]
- Learn WPF MVVM[5]

To be published

- Learn Docker
- Learn Kubernetes
- Learn Unit Testing
- Learn Universal Windows

---

[1] https://leanpub.com/netcore
[2] https://leanpub.com/aspnetmvc
[3] https://leanpub.com/learnmeteor
[4] https://leanpub.com/micro
[5] https://leanpub.com/learnwpf

www.ingramcontent.com/pod-product-compliance
Lightning Source LLC
Chambersburg PA
CBHW071436180526
45170CB00001B/364